The miner's home

Anne Witherington

This book is about a home in the North East of England in 1913. It was the home of a coal miner and his family. In the North East miners were called pitmen.

You do not have to read this book from beginning to end. You can just turn to the pages that interest you.

Contents

The miner's cottage

The miner and his family lived in a cottage.
It had two rooms downstairs and an attic upstairs.

⬆ Pit cottages were built near to the pit where the men worked.

There were lots of cottages built in a row.

Every cottage had a front garden and a back yard.
Downstairs there was a parlour and a kitchen.
Sometimes there was a pantry which was part of
the kitchen. A miner, his wife and their children
lived in one of these small cottages.

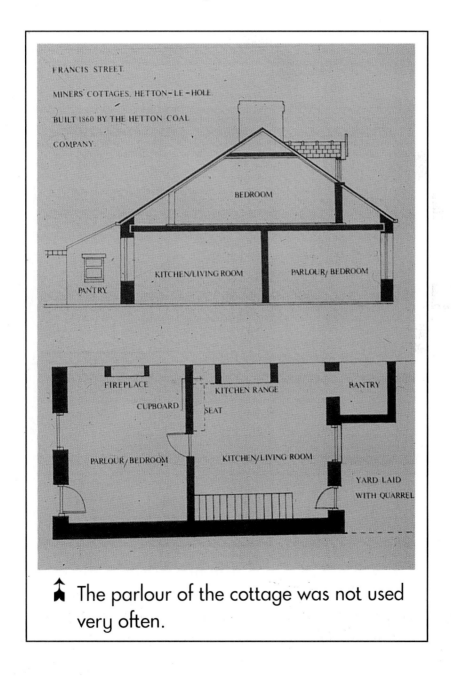

FRANCIS STREET

MINERS' COTTAGES, HETTON-LE-HOLE

BUILT 1860 BY THE HETTON COAL

COMPANY

BEDROOM

KITCHEN/LIVING ROOM

PARLOUR/ BEDROOM

PANTRY

FIREPLACE

KITCHEN RANGE

PANTRY

CUPBOARD

SEAT

PARLOUR/ BEDROOM

KITCHEN/LIVING ROOM

YARD LAID

WITH QUARREL

The parlour of the cottage was not used
very often.

The kitchen and pantry

The kitchen was a very busy room.
The family used it for cooking, washing,
ironing, bathing and eating.
It was even used
as a bedroom.

⬆ The fire warmed the house,
cooked the food, heated the
water and dried the clothes.

The fresh foods were kept in the pantry. The big kitchen table was scrubbed twice a day with green soap and it was scrubbed once a week with salt to keep it clean.

The bed kept in the cupboard was called a dess bed and was used by the older children or family visitors.

⬆ A ladder went through a hole in the ceiling to the attic.

The parlour

The parlour was the best room.
Children were only allowed in at special times.
It was also mum and dad's bedroom.
It had lots of furniture in it.

⬆ The parlour was only used for funerals and other special days.

⬆ Girls embroidered samplers at school.

The miner bought good quality furniture. The chair seats and sofa were stuffed with horse hair which was prickly to sit on. They had a carpet on the floor.

On special days the family might have a sing song round the harmonium.

⬆ This is called a half tester bed because it only has a canopy at one end.

⬆ Mum washed herself at the washstand.

The attic

The children slept in the attic.

They could sleep on mattresses on the floor.

Four children slept on one mattress.

They kept each other warm.

⬆ The children did not have any toys in the attic.
This picture was taken many years ago.

The children had woollen blankets on the beds.
The heat from the kitchen fire helped to keep
the room warm.
A curtain was hung across the room
to separate the boys from the girls.

⬆ The chamber pot or
guzunder was used at night.

⬆ They used a candle to
light up the room.

9

The front garden

The miner grew vegetables and flowers in the garden.
The gardens were long and narrow.

The miner grew the vegetables and his family used them to make soups and dinners. Some miners built pigeon lofts or greenhouses in their gardens. Some even built a pig sty.

⬆ The miner worked in the garden when he was not working at the pit.

The back yard

On fine days, the miner's wife did the washing in the backyard. The coal house and the netty were in the back yard too. The netty was the toilet.

⬆ The netty had no water to flush it, so people called midden men emptied it at night.

The miner's wife did her washing in a big tub
called a poss tub. She filled it with hot water and
used a poss stick to bash the dirt out of the clothes.
Then she used a mangle to squeeze the water out.

A tin bath was kept in the back yard.
This was taken into the kitchen and filled with
hot water on bath nights.

⬆ The mangle and poss tub were kept in the back yard.

The back lane

The back lane was a busy place because everybody used the back door to go into the houses.
The children played games in the back lane.

⬆ The washing was hung across the back lane in fine weather. This picture was taken many years ago.

The fish seller, the fruit seller, the midden men and the rag and bone man all brought their carts into the back lane. When the carts arrived the women had to take their washing down.

⬆ The women met for a chat in the back lane. This picture was taken many years ago.

Glossary of words used in this book

Attic   An attic is a room in the roof of a house.

Canopy   A canopy is like a small roof over a bed.

Chamber pot   A chamber pot is a potty which is used as a toilet.

Dess bed   A dess bed is a bed that folds up to look like a cupboard or a chest of drawers.

Half tester   A half tester bed had two posts which held a curtain up around the bed.

Harmonium   A harmonium is a musical instrument that looks like a small piano.

Mangle   A mangle was a machine that was used to get water out of clothes. It had two rollers.

Midden men   The midden men worked at night and cleaned out the toilets.

Miner   A miner is a person who works under the ground.

Netty   A netty was an outside toilet. It had no water in it.

Pantry   A pantry was a small room leading from the kitchen. Crockery and fresh foods were kept in the pantry.

Parlour   A parlour was the best room in the house.

Poss stick   A poss stick was a heavy wooden stick. It helped to get the dirt out of clothes.

Poss tub   A poss tub was a large wooden bucket. Clothes were washed in it.

Rag and bone man   A rag and bone man collected things that people did not want. He took them away to sell.

Sampler   A sampler was a picture or some fancy writing. It was made by sewing.

Wash stand   A wash stand was a table. On the table there was a bowl and jug.